INTRODUCTION

The history. Copenhagen, the capital of Denmark, located on the eastern tip of Sjælland Island, sits in a strategic position, separated from Sweden by the narrow strait of the Øresund. In ancient times the city had a smaller port (Havn, in Danish). Documents tell us that this town of fishermen and merchants, after having taken the Latinized name of Hafnia, was ceded in 1167 by King Valdemar to Absalon, the Bishop of Roskilde. The bishop lost no time in fortifying the small island of Slotsholmen which today lies in the center of the city. The new fortress was originally built to defend the area from pirate raids but soon became a strategic stronghold, feared and coveted by many powers. It was destroyed a first time in 1249 by armies from Lubeck and a second time in 1369 by the Hanseatic League forces. In spite of the devastation caused by wars, the city continued to grow and prosper; it is no chance that it was known as Købmandehavn, "the merchants' port".

The amount of traffic coming through the port was so great that it led several rulers to attempt the annexation of the city from the Bishop of Roskilde's jurisdiction and from the raids of the Hanseatic League which considered Copenhagen a dangerous rival in commercial trading. Finally, in the first half of the fifteenth century, Henry VII of Pomerania moved into the newly rebuilt fortress and from here, as well as from the nearby Helsingør Castle, he was able to levy a toll on all the ships passing through the strait, making Copenhagen the flourishing capital of his kingdom. Already under Christian I of Oldenburg, a university was established and the city began to take on a precise plan. It wasn't, however, until a century later with Christian IV (1588-1648), who went down in history as the "Architect

King", that Copenhagen reached its full artistic, cultural, economic and architectural splendor. The island of Slotsholmen was enlarged by draining a canal, making way for the erection of the magnificent castle of Christiansborg, today's noble descendent of the previous ancient fortress. In this period splendid buildings were constructed along the central axis of the Strøget which was already starting to assume its present-day form. New port facilities and mighty fortifications enclosed the entire city to the south and east in a star formation. In the direction of the sea, the city was protected by an invincible walled barrier whose center was located in the pentagonal bastion of the Kastellet. Instead, to the west, three large artificial lakes: Sankt Jørgens Sø, Peblinge Sø and Sortedamns Sø guaranteed adequate protection against possible land attacks.

Such was the scope of Christian IV's projects that in many cases only his successors would witness their completion. This was the period of development for the areas of Nyboder, Frederiksstad (with its orthogonal streets that would converge in the square of Amalienborg in the 1700s) and Christianshavn, which grew up on the sandy shores of Amager Island. Nicolai Eigtved, architect and favorite of Frederick IV, undoubtedly played a key role in the second phase of expansion that took place in the mid-1700s. In the meantime, however, Copenhagen's destiny

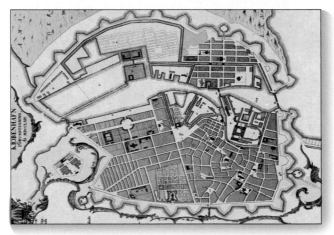

seemed directed towards less grandiose objectives. The terrible plague of 1711-1712 which decimated the population was followed by a series of devastating fires, including the truly catastrophic ones of 1728 and 1795. Finally, the bombardments inflicted by the British fleet in 1801 and 1807 (the first one caused a new, terrible blaze) put Copenhagen's economy and its very life in question.

However, in the mid 1800s significant changes began to be discernible: wide areas of the city had been de-militarized while a good portion of the walls were torn down to make room for new residential districts. At the same time, green spaces were singled out for preservation within the city center, just one example of how careful attention to the environment has always been part of Danish culture. Soon, however, even the new residential areas proved insufficient in the face of a strong demographic growth which began in the first half of the nineteenth century but became especially noticeable after 1850. Thus at the opening of the twentieth century Copenhagen boasted nearly half a million people, a growing industrial sector, a very busy port and a careful building program which resulted in the urban plan's concentric development.

These two historic maps illustrate the great urban development that took place during the seventeenth century and changed the face of Copenhagen. Notice the building of fortifications that protected the city on the side of Amager island. The great complex of Christiansborg would be built at the center of this plan.

HANS CHRISTIAN ANDERSEN

Among the most celebrated men of modern Denmark, Hans Christian Andersen has become a true symbol of his country together with one of the most melancholy creations of his fantasy, the Little Mermaid. His *Fairy Tales* bring wonderful dreams to life, concealing lessons and profound meanings in a world of fantasy.

Yet this famous author's life was never in the least like a fairy tale. Born a poor shoemaker's son in Odense in 1805, Andersen never received regular schooling. At age fourteen, with the death of his father, he came to Copenhagen to seek his fortune on the stage. In spite of the generous assistance of several patrons which allowed him to finish his studies, he was not spared disappointments: his poems, novels and travel books inspired by his visits to many different European countries (from England to Turkey, from Spain to Italy and Greece) never met with success. Andersen was never able to make a go of his theatrical career and, as for his sentimental attachments, these brought him only bitter disillusionment. Perhaps it was just such negative experiences that gave his writing that distinc-

tive veil of melancholy that would be one of the keys to the universal success of his real masterpiece, the *Fairy Tales* (1835-1872). In this work humor, poetry, fantasy and education are interwoven to generate such immortal characters as the Ugly Duckling, the Lead Soldier, the Little Match Girl and, above all, the Little Mermaid who is perhaps the one dearest to the Danes. After Andersen's death in Copenhagen in 1875, his fairy tale characters would establish and immortalize his fame the world over.

The Royal Family. No history of Copenhagen can be considered complete without giving proper attention to the history of the Danish monarchy which has always represented one of the fundamental elements of the nation's identity. The present queen, Margaret II, has undoubtedly won devotion and a special place in the hearts of her subjects. Being liberal in her ways, she is thought of as one of the people.

In 1953 the law excluding female succession to the throne was repealed and in 1972, when she had just turned thirty-two, she succeeded her father Frederick IX. With her husband, the Prince Consort Henrik (who is of French noble descent) she has two sons: Frederick, heir to the throne, born in 1968 a year after her wedding, and Joachim born in 1969. The royal family usually resides at Amalienborg but has always shown itself to be deeply democratic and close to the people, appearing in public even for unofficial occasions.

The Oldenburg dynasty to which Margaret belongs is one of the oldest ruling houses in all of Europe and its origins date back to the eleventh century. From the mid-fifteenth century and without interruption, the Oldenburgs have sat on the Danish throne. In fact, it was Christian of Oldenburg, son of Theodoric the Lucky and Edvige of Holstein, who ensured the success of his lineage by becoming sovereign of Denmark (with the name Christian I), Norway and Sweden as well as Count of Holstein and Duke of Schleswig. His reign marked the end of what is conventionally thought of as the Middle Ages in Denmark; under his descendants, the whole country would grow economically, culturally, artistically and even politically. In 1849 Denmark received its first constitution with the support of Frederick VII. Since then, and with the new Grundlov (Constitution) of June 5, 1953, the monarchy, although it has remained hereditary, is called upon to exercise only executive powers while the unicameral Parliament performs the legislative functions and the courts form the judicial body.

Queen Margaret and her family (below left, Frederick, the heir to the throne) during some official ceremonies.

Copenhagen today. *After the Second World War the idea of "reconstructive restoration" became widespread, while in the 1960s urban renewal of large areas of the city, especially Nyhavn, saved them from a progressively run-down state. Even the port district, which had been decaying from the reduced volume of maritime traffic, received a new vital impetus from these renewal programs. Today at last Copenhagen is an airy city, rich in green parks. Imbued during the day with a tranquil and orderly atmosphere that reflects the excellent quality of life, the city can suddenly come alive in the late night hours. The capital of Denmark is living a happy period of great rebirth which is underscored by the vitality and creativity of its people. So the name coined for this city which was elected the cultural capital of Europe in 1996 is still valid: Copenhagen, the Paris of the North.*

Faces, clothing, meeting places, customs, evocations, daily scenes in the dynamic yet harmonious Copenhagen of today: everything here takes place according to an ordered lifestyle which is creative as well as being distinguished by a joyous serenity.

THE GOLDEN BOOK
COPENHAGEN
AND ENVIRONS

MAP OF THE CITY

TEXT BY
PATRIZIA FABBRI

Project and editorial conception: Casa Editrice Bonechi
Publication Manager: Monica Bonechi
Picture research: Monica Bonechi
Graphic design and cover: Manuela Ranfagni
Make-up: Alberto Douglas Scotti
Editing: Patrizia Fabbri, Simonetta Giorgi
Map: Stefano Benini
Text: Patrizia Fabbri
Translation: Miranda MacPhail

Printed in Italy by Centro Stampa Editoriale Bonechi.

Photographs:
Carrebye Billedarkiv, Lyngby: *pages 3 above, 4 below right and left, 11 below right, 12 above and left, 15 below, 21 above, 27 below, 35 below right, 37-38, 39 below left, 40 above left, 42, 45 below, 46 centre right, 48 above, 52 above, 53 above, 57 above, centre and right, 58, 60 below, 61, 64 above left, 66 above, 67 above right, centre right and below, 68, 70 above, 72 above and below left, 73 below, 76, 77 above, 78 below, 79, 84/85, 88-89, 90;* Maurizio Fraschetti, Rome: *pages 13 above, 33 above, 40 centre and below, 62 below, 64 above right;* Andrea Innocenti, Florence: *pages 28 above, 46 in the middle of the box, 48 below, 49 above right and left;* Nathalie Krag-Gianni Giorgi, Florence: *pages 3 below, 11 above right, 20 above, 21 below right and left, 22 above, 23 above (in the box), 43, 46 above, 50, 74-75;* Andrea Pistolesi, Florence: *pages 8, 9, 10, 11 below left, 13 below, 14 above, 17-19, 24/25, 32 below right and left, 44, 45 above, 56, 86-87, 92-93;* Ghigo Roli, Florence: *pages 6 above, left and centre, and below right, 7, 63;* 2 maj, Copenhagen: *pages 5, 6 above right, centre and below left and centre, 11 above left, 12 below right and left, 14 below, 15 above right and left, 16, 20 below, 22/23, 23 centre and below, 26, 27 above, 28 centre and below right and left, 29-31, 32 above, 33 below, 34, 35 above and below left (in the box), 36, 39 above and below right, 46 centre left (above in the box) and below right and left (below in the box), 47, 49 below, 51, 52/53, 54-55, 57 below left, 59, 60 above and centre, 62 above, 64 centre and below right and left, 65, 66 below right and left, 67 above left and centre left, 69, 70 centre and below right and left, 71, 72 below right, 73 above, 78 above, 82-83;* Mikkel Østergaard-Billed huset: *page 41 above;* Jørgen Schytte-Billed huset: *page 41 below.*

Photographs on pages 80-81, courtesy of Louisiana Museum of Modern Art, Humlebæk, Denmark.

Photographs on pages 62 centre, 77 below, 91, courtesy of Francesco Giannoni.

ISBN 88-476-0224-6

* * *

A fine view of the City Square, with the impressive City Hall building and, left, the Palace Hotel.
Above, a detail of the City Hall tower with the bronze statue of traditional "Lur players".

RÅDHUSPLADSEN

The great **City Square** (*Rådhuspladsen*) forms the very heart of historic Copenhagen, although it was only built as we see it today in the early 1900s, at the same time as the City Hall. Originally designed in a shell-like shape, its form has been lost in the transformations made to accomodate the needs of modern traffic and public transportation. However, in the square's complex composition, the whole effect is still incredibly beautiful.

To the right of City Hall stands the famous *Dragon Fountain* (*Dragespringvandet*), a bronze work (1901) by Thorvald Bindesbøll and Joakim Skovgaard. Nearby is the *stone* which represents the zero mile for the whole Danish road system. Moving right, the entrance to the green *gardens of H.C. Andersens Boulevard* is marked by an expressive statue of the fairy tale author. To the left of City Hall a column holds up the *bronze sculpture of the Lurblæserne* (or players of the "lur", an ancient musical instrument used by Nordic peoples up until the sixth century BC), a work (1914) by Siegfried Wagner. Facing onto the square, the *Richshuset* is famous for its unusual barometer that predicts good or bad weather by the appearance of small figures: either a woman on a bicycle or a woman with an umbrella. The *Palace Hotel* also fronts onto the square. Built in the most elegant eclectic style by Anton Rosen between 1910 and 1912, the façade tower's decoration was obviously inspired by the lines and volumes of the City Hall, undoubtedly the square's most important building. Topped by the *Rådhustårnet*, a tower ending in an elegant spire that soars more than one hundred meters above the ground, the **City Hall** (*Rådhuset*) shows clear references to Italian architecture especially to Siena's City Hall and more generally to Italian and Scandinavian Renaissance prototypes. This can be seen especially in the stern battlements as well as

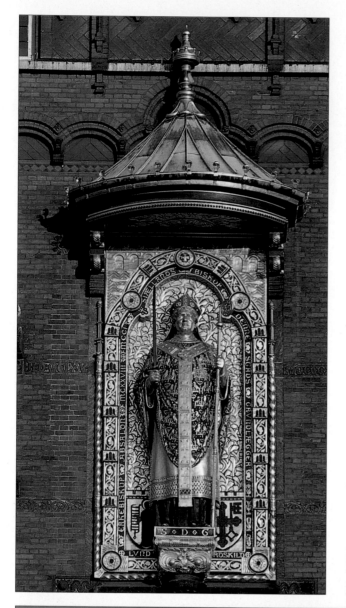

in the brick façade where, over the entrance, rises the *statue* of the city's warring founder, Bishop Absalon. In 1888 a competition was held to design this building on a site where previous structures had been systematically destroyed by the fires that had repeatedly swept through the city. Martin Nyrop won the competition and his project was successfully carried out between 1892 and 1905. From the roof above, six *statues* of Renaissance sentinels seem to stand guard over the Hall, observing the people leaving and entering.

Inside the *Rådhuset*, an elegant atrium leads to the spectacular *astronomical clock*, a monumental work by Jens Olsen (1955) who gave it as many as twelve quadrants indicating the time in every part of the world as well as a full series of astronomical data that calculates all the planets' positions. The City Hall proper, rectangular in design, is composed of a series of finely furnished *rooms* arranged around a *Council Hall*. Behind, the picturesque *Flowered Courtyard* has been embellished by the addition of the *Bears' Fountain* (*Bjørnespringvandet*). As for the area off the square, the streets nearby are elegant and lively, especially at night when lights and sounds combine to give an electric yet chic atmosphere that seduces anyone passing by.

Left, the statue of Absalon – Bishop of Roskilde and famous founder of Copenhagen – on the façade above the City Hall's main entrance.
Below, the city's coat-of-arms is set between two Renaissance sentinels on the roof of the City Hall.

Above, the enormous courtyard at the entrance of City Hall.
Right, the Palace Hotel's eclectic façade.
Lower left, the sculptural elegance of the Dragon Fountain embellishes the square.
Lower right, the statue of Hans Christian Andersen sits at the entrance to the gardens.

Views illustrating the lively night-time atmosphere of the area around City Square. Among the streets still jammed with people, one can't mistake the entrance to Tivoli Park which is lit by a myriad of small lights. Not far away stand the huge round structure of the Domus Circus (left) and the colorful façade of the Palads Cinema (lower left).

STRØGET

One of the main arteries crossing the city is the famous pedestrian way, the **Strøget**, which runs from the City Square to the *Kongens Nytorv* and is formed by a long succession of streets and squares (*Frederiksberggade, Nygade, Vimmelskaftet, Gammeltorv, Nytorv, Amagertorv, Østergade*). The Strøget is characterized by decidedly commercial activity (a vast array of shops line the street) and by its substantially uniform architecture which is the result of eighteenth and nineteenth century reconstructions after the devastation wrought by several fires. The Strøget can be considered the city's "parlor" and many of the buildings facing onto it are of interest. Among them the old *Metropol Cinema*, today the headquarters of a department store, was built by Anton Rosen in 1912 and is still considered one of the best examples of the Danish *Art Nouveau* style. The Neoclassical *Domhuset*, built in 1815 as the City Hall and Justice Department, is fronted by an elegant colonnade in the Ionic style. The *Helligåndshuset*, perhaps the oldest building in Copenhagen, and the Church of the Holy Spirit represent the last vestiges of a fifteenth-century monastery of the same name. Finally the *Mathias Hansens Gård*, built in the 1600s in the Renaissance style, is the commercial headquarters for the prestigious *Royal Copenhagen Porcelain Factory*, founded in

Right, one of Nytorv's most characteristic landmarks, the early twentieth-century newsstand with a copper roof, also served as a telephone booth.
Below, the elegant bronze Fountain of Charity marks the center of Gammeltorv.

One of the monuments that the people of
Copenhagen hold most dear is the Storks
Fountain, set at the center of Amagertorv
(left). In Medieval times this square with its
ornamental paving was the site of a market
and even today it is surrounded by elegant
shops as well as by crowded bars and
restaurants. Another pleasant meeting
point is in Gråbrødretorv, the historic
Square of the Franciscans (right), under
the shade of the tall plain tree.

1775. The production has been the
direct property of the · Danish
Crown since 1779 and today is
famous worldwide; in fact on the
building's first floor there is a small
museum that illustrates the history
and tradition of the renowned
Porcelænsfabrik.

Along the almost two-kilometer-
long central axis of the Strøget,
there are also magnificent bronze
fountains like the seventeenth-century *Fountain of Charity (Caritas
Springvandet)*, rebuilt by Hans Teg-
ner in 1890, and the famous *Fountain of the Storks (Storkespringvan-
det)* which is a symbol of the centuries-old relationship between the
Danes and these lovely birds that
nest among the chimneys.

RUNDETÅRN

I n 1642, King Christian IV decided to donate an astronomical observatory to the University of Copenhagen. Thus the **Rundetårn** was built: a round brick tower, about 36 meters high, where the king's name is still clearly visible on the façade. The most famous Danish astronomer Tycho Brahe carried out his studies at the Rundetårn but it wasn't until 1929 that the present rotating dome with a telescope was added. A spectacular *spiral ramp* leads to the top of the tower. About 209 meters long, the ramp was visited in 1716 by the Russian Czar Peter the Great, on horseback, with the carriage of the Czarina Catherine behind. The monumental structure also serves — improperly — as the bell tower for the adjacent **Trinity Church** (*Trinitatis Kirke*), which was also begun by Christian IV for the University students but was only completed in 1656. The church interior houses many fine decorations, all dating from after the blaze of 1728. Particularly noteworthy are pieces like the Baroque *high altar* by Friedrich Ehbisch (1731), the Rococo-style *clock* made by the Danish artisan Peter Michael Abel in 1757, and the wonderful Baroque *organ front*, also dating from 1731 while the organ itself was built in 1956.

NICOLAI KIRKEBYGNING

I n 1795 a fire destroyed the **Church of Saint Nicholas** (*Nicolai Kirkebygning*) located right in the heart of the city. The building, erected in the thirteenth century, had already undergone substantial renovations in the course of the 1500s when a tower had been added. After destruction by fire in the 1700s, this tower was the first part to be rebuilt, in the nineteenth century, using the original plans. The rest of the building would have to wait until 1915 when Hans Christian Amberg undertook reconstruction using decidedly more modern drawings. Today the spaces of the building are used for temporary exhibitions.

Left, the Rundetårn.
Right, from top: the elegant spiral ramp, the organ and a view of the nave in Trinity Church.
On the following page, the Church of Saint Nicholas.

Above, a view of the Kongens Nytorv with the equestrian monument of Christian V, the king who commissioned the building of the square.

KONGENS NYTORV

Almost as if to mark Copenhagen's historic center or to serve as a dramatic precursor of what would become the monumental area of Amalienborg, the **Kongens Nytorv** or "new King's Square" was commissioned by Christian V in 1672. Originally inspired by French city planning, it has become one of the city's main thoroughfares, facing on to the picturesque bay of *Nyhavn*.

Even today the august patron seems to watch over his creation: an *equestrian statue of Christian V* by Abraham Cesar Lamoureux (1688) stands in the middle of the square, surrounded by a ring of green trees. The important buildings lining the *Kongens Nytorv* soon made this area one of the city's most elegant quarters. In the early twentieth century, Copenhagen's high-life found a chic meeting point at the *Hotel d'Angleterre*, situated to the right of where the *Strøget* enters the square. Just north, the seventeenth-century Thott family palace (*Thotts Palæ*) built in the Baroque period was later remodeled in the Neoclassical style. The magnificent *Charlottenborg* residence was built along the canal in the period between 1672 and 1683 for Ulrik F. Gyldenløve, son of Frederick III. It was designed in a typical Dutch Baroque style, symmetrically laid out around a central courtyard. The large, well-tended garden that attracted great admiration was acquired, together with the house, in 1700 by Carlotta Amalia, Christian V's widow. Since 1754, it has served as the seat of the *Kongelige Kunstakademi*, the *Royal Academy of Fine Arts*, founded by Frederick V.

Above, facing onto the Kongens Nytorv is the severe and majestic façade of the Royal Theater which is a key institution in the history of Danish theater.
Left, the harmonious white façade of the Hotel d'Angleterre.

On the following page, above: the Nyhavn canal, that extends as far as the Kongens Nytorv, is seen here with the elegant Charlottenborg residence in the background.

Two other elegant buildings face onto the square: *Harsdorffs Palæ*, a neoclassical construction erected in 1779-1780 as the home of the renowned Danish architect whose name it bears today; and, above all, *Det Kongelige Teater* or *Royal Theater*. The temple of Danish drama, this austere and stately building with its elements of eclecticism was designed between 1872 and 1874 by Jens Vilhelm Dahlerup and Ove Petersen. The main theater has a seating capacity of 1500 and is sumptuously decorated. In 1931 Holger Jacobsen added a second theater — called the *Nye Scene* or "New Stage", with 1050 seats — on the other side of the *Tordenskjoldsgade*.

COPENHAGEN ON TWO WHEELS

The bicycle is an essential element of Danish tradition and daily life. A great number of Danes use bicycles, with healthy enthusiasm, all year round without being discouraged even by winter's frostiest days. Genuine preference for this means of transportation is demonstrated by the widespread network of bicycle paths (more than 5000 kilometers) that runs across the whole country.

Undoubtedly tied to the Danes' great sensitivity towards environmental issues, particularly efficient organizations promote the use of bicycles. One example is Copenhagen's regular **City Bike** service that puts a bicycle at anyone's disposal. The inhabitants' widespread use of bicycles has resulted in Copenhagen having clean air, less noise and hardly any traffic jams — most unusual for a large European capital.

NYHAVN

I n the second half of the 1600s, a new port able to meet the massive growth of commercial traffic became necessary and so a large basin-canal which ran into the heart of the city was built. The **Nyhavn** or "New Port" was active for many years but in this century, after a long period of recession, it was abandoned to a sad decline. Today, thanks to a decisive move for its renovation, *Nyhavn* has become a picturesque quarter with many restaurants and cafes. It still preserves some signs of its past history: for example a number of tattoo parlors are found here and, still on the water, many docked boats have been made into bars. This new pleasant atmosphere is framed on both sides of the canal by close rows of characteristic three to four storey buildings dating from the sixteenth and seventeenth centuries. Once homes, warehouses or armories, these constructions provide interesting examples of old, historic building styles: brick façades are alternated with Neoclassical buildings, Baroque homes stand next to Flemish constructions, and three eighteenth-century houses that hosted Hans Christian Andersen at different times are still visible. On the northern side of the canal rises the imposing *Arsenal*, built in 1650 and converted, in the twentieth century, into an original and charming hotel. A large *ship-lighthouse*, the *Fyrskib XVII*, is anchored on the canal's southern bank. Inaugurated in 1896, it was a fundamental reference point for Northern European sailors and today serves as an interesting and unusual museum that documents the difficult lives they led at sea. In front of the port entrance, a unique *monument* in the form of a giant anchor commemorates the Danish sailors who died for their country during the Second World War.

Here and on the following pages: views of Nyhavn's basin and canal, lined by buildings constructed one right against the other and crowded by boats of all sizes. This quarter hosts a great number of very popular bars and restaurants.

NYHAVN'S SIGNS

Among the peculiarities of the *Nyhavn* basin-canal area, one that won't go unnoticed is the great presence of signs. Brightly colored, hand-worked, all very visible: they call attention to the many attractions that this lively quarter of Copenhagen has in store for visitors.

CHRISTIANSBORG

I n the historic center of Copenhagen, a sea inlet was dug to make a canal (*Slotsholmskanalen*) thus creating the island of *Slotsholmen* where the mighty castle of **Christiansborg** is located. The initial phase of construction consisted of the fortress built by Archbishop Absalon in 1167 which was first destroyed in 1249 by armies from Lubeck and again in 1369 by the Hanseatic League. Twenty years afterwards, the Archbishop of Roskilde rebuilt the castle which was later chosen by Henry VII of Pomerania as his royal residence. Soon, however, the building proved unsuited to the growing needs of the Court. Thus in 1687 Christian V commissioned from David Elias Hauser its complete renovation which was completed under Christian VI. The result of these works was a complex of three hundred and fifty rooms, inaugurated in 1766 for the wedding of Christian VII with Caroline Mathilda, princess of Great Britain. After that time, however, the royal residence was continually damaged by fires: devastated by flames in 1794 and further damaged the next year by a

Views of the stately Christiansborg complex. The equestrian monument to Frederick VII (1873) stands in front of the entrance from the Slotplads.

blaze that swept across the entire city, the castle was demolished in 1803. It was rebuilt in 1828 according to Christian Frederik Hansen's Neoclassical design. However, in spite of all the scrupulously-adopted preventive measures, the new castle fell victim once again to fire in 1884. The present three-storey building, designed in 1907 by Thorvald Jørgensen, is topped by a high *tower* with a copper spire and is arranged around a large central *courtyard*. To get there one first has to pass over the *Marmorbroen* (Marble Bridge), cross the courtyard with the large *riding stables* (*Christiansborg Ridebane*) and pass the *equestrian statue of Christian IX* (1927). Today the south and east wings of the complex are taken up by the Parliament (*Folketing*), government offices and the Supreme Court. The north wing is reserved for *ceremonial rooms* which have elegant furnishings and priceless works of art (among which there are many marble sculptures by Thorvaldsen), not to mention magnificent *tapestries*. Among the latter, of particular interest are the seventeenth-century Flemish tapestries attributed to Berend van der Eichen that decorate the immense *Hall of the Knights* (*Riddersalen*). Special mention should be made of the eighty thousand volumes that make up the Queen's private library that is located in this wing. Very little has come down to us of the site's previous buildings that were destroyed by fire. Remains

Danish flags are flown from the high, copper-roofed spire that tops the Christiansborg Castle. Lower left, a view of the wing facing onto the Stable Courtyard, with a statue of Christian IX. The stately building that serves as the seat of Parliament (above, the façade that opens onto the Slotplads) is also remarkable for its elegant rooms and fine decorations which often include royal insignia.

One of the castle's many large and well-lit rooms; the Parliamentary Chamber.

of the more ancient fortress's foundations were uncovered in the early 1900s on the site of the inner courtyard which is still surrounded by the Baroque colonnade (*Ridebaneanlægget*) built under Christian VI. The magnificent *stables* by Nicolai Eigtved are situated next to an interesting **Carriage Museum** (*Karetmuseet*). In 1767, under the reign of Christian VII, Nicolas Henri Jardin designed the *Court Theater* which has since been turned into the **Museum of Theater History** (*Teatermuseet*). Lastly the more ancient *Lange Tøjhus*, the enormous arsenal erected for Christian IV between 1598 and 1604, is located to the left of the great castle. It, too, has been converted into a **museum** which is devoted, not surprisingly given its site, to Danish military history.

THE COURT CHAPEL

The fury of Christiansborg's last devastating fire spared the Neoclassical **Court Chapel** (*Slotskirken*). Added in 1826 to the castle's north wing (to which it is joined by a roofed passage), it was designed by Christian Frederik Hansen and decorated with *statues of evangelists and angels* by Bertel Thorvaldsen. Today its hall, fronted by a monumental colonnade, is used for concerts on account of the perfect acoustics.

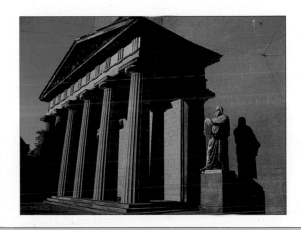

THE THORVALDSEN MUSEUM

Bertel Thorvaldsen (1770-1844), considered modern Denmark's greatest sculptor, was the son of an Icelandic immigrant who pushed him with determination towards an artistic career to the point of enrolling him at the Academy of Fine Arts. A **mausoleum** dedicated to Thorvaldsen and his work was built (1839-1848) by Gottlieb Bindesbøll on a site next to Christiansborg where the sculptor wished to be buried in a simple grave. The façade, dominated by a quadriga (or four-horse-drawn chariot) donated by King Christian VIII, has five great doorways that lead to the *museum*. Here several original marble pieces are shown alongside many plaster copies of Thorvaldsen's works; these were either made by the sculptor himself or, after his death, by other artists under the supervision of Hermann Vilhelm Bissen. The rich collection of paintings and antiquities that the artist had willed to the museum is displayed on the first floor.

The mausoleum dedicated to Bertel Thorvaldsen, with its polychrome frieze running along the exterior façade, faces onto the canal surrounding the island of Christiansborg. Many of the great sculptor's works are still preserved here.

Views of the superb Royal Library

THE ROYAL LIBRARY

Close by Christiansborg but housed in a separate building, the **Kongelige Biblotek**, with its fifty-five thousand manuscripts, four million papers and paintings, and two and a half million books, is the largest library in Scandinavia and proof of the keen interest that Danish sovereigns have always shown towards library collections. Housed today in a building designed by Hans Jørgen Holm in 1906, on the site of an ancient shipping dock, the Royal Library was originally founded by King Frederick III in 1670. Surrounded by a magnificent garden with a small lake, the building combines Gothic forms and Baroque elements. Here interesting documents written by famous Danish authors are preserved, authors ranging from Tycho Brahe to Søren Kierkegaard, from Hans Christian Andersen to Karen Blixen.

BØRSEN

S ituated not far from Christiansborg, this Dutch Renaissance-style building housed the **Stock Exchange** until 1974 since when it has been the headquarters of the Danish Chamber of Commerce. It is not renowned so much for its shape — a large rectangle — for its brick façade or for the tree-lined ramp which in old times allowed carriages to drive up to the first floor above the commodities warehouse. Rather, it is known for its unusual *tower*: the tails of three dragons symbolizing Denmark, Norway and Sweden twist together to form a kind of spiral arrow soaring towards the sky. The *Børsen*, too, is a creation of the Architect King, Christian IV, who in the first half of the seventeenth century commissioned the building from Lourens and Hans van Steenwinckel. In the eighteenth and nineteenth centuries the whole structure underwent substantial restoration, including the rebuilding of the tower (1775-1777) and the renovation of the great hall (1857-1858) that would house the Stock Exchange.

HOLMENS KIRKE

T he origins of this church are very curious indeed: the original building was constructed in 1563 as an anchor foundry and only in 1619 was it converted, on Christian IV's wish, into a chapel for sailors of the Danish fleet. The **Holmens Kirke**'s present appearance can be traced back to the substantial changes carried out between 1641 and 1643 to make it a more suitable place of worship. Today it is still the Navy's official church. It is also known as the Royal Chapel and for this reason in 1967 the wedding of the future queen Margaret was held here.

VOR FRELSERS KIRKE

A nother church that has played a very important role in the life and history of Copenhagen is the **Vor Frelsers Kirke**. A Baroque red brick building consecrated to the Redeemer, it is located in one of the oldest areas of *Christianshavn*, near *Skt. Annæ Gade*. It is easily identified by the copper tower, 93 meters high, built between 1747 and 1752, which culminates in a single winding spire. At its top is a statue of the Redeemer that can be reached via a spiral staircase running up the inside of the spire. Erected between 1682 and 1696 by Lambert van Haven, the church has a Greek cross plan inside and houses fine works in marble and wood dating from the sixteenth and seventeenth centuries.

Left, the elegant Børsen with its long façades, characteristic dormer windows and distinctive spiral tower.
Upper right, facing onto the Borsgraven canal, the Holmens Kirke rises above the bust of Bishop Fog who headed the Sjælland Diocese in the nineteenth century.
Right, the unique tower of the Church of the Savior in the Christianshavn district.

An aerial view of Christianshavn showing the district's unique urban plan.
On the following page, images of daily life along the canals which are particularly numerous in this district.

CHRISTIANSHAVN

A large moving bridge, the *Knippelsbro*, joins the center of Copenhagen with the northern part of *Amager Island* and in particular with the **Christianshavn** port district. Although it has become part of the city's urban area, the district still preserves its own unique identity. This is due in part to the massive star-shaped fortifications laid out in the eighteenth century which still contain the area on three sides while the fourth is protected by the wide *Stadsgraven* moat. Such strong boundaries give a clear idea of King Christian IV's original project to make this area into an invincible fortress. However, free commerce and the need for another well-equipped port eventually won out over any strategy. The king's initial project was simplified and wide streets, alternating with narrower ones, were built to make way for further development:

houses, shops, warehouses and ships' docks. Indeed, one of the largest shipyards in the country was located here.

After a period of abandonment, Christianshavn has been revitalized in recent times. Today characteristic houses — some of the oldest date back even to the sixteenth and seventeenth centuries — overlook the canal and the pleasant parks that have been laid out on the sites of partially converted fortifications. This gentrification has led to the restoration of other buildings as well, like the monumental **Vor Frelsers Kirke**, a church overlooking the district from its own pier. Another curious site in this area is the *B & W Museet* located in *Strandgade*: it is a large exhibition of the different periods of motor shipping in Denmark and around the world.

THE "FREE CITY" OF CHRISTIANIA

One of the more recent and controversial "institutions" of Christianshavn is the free city of **Christiania**, a real social laboratory that deals with many complex issues. The hippies that founded *Christiania* in 1971 took over old army barracks and preached a free life, an obedience to ecological values as well as a return to the earth, needless to say all with a good dose of transgression. Ever since its foundation the community, which today counts about a thousand members, has always been at the center of controversy.

A large complex of buildings — all connected among themselves but each with a separate entrance — houses the vast, prized collections of the Nationalmuseet, the most prestigious museum of Danish civilization and culture.

NATIONALMUSEET

The **Nationalmuseet** was founded in 1897 by the unification of several prestigious sources: the ancient collection of Ole Worm (who died in 1654, but his collection represented the real heart of the original museum); precious artifacts from the *Kongelige Museum for Nordiske Oldsager*; interesting historical and ethnographic collections; a remarkable number of coins and medallions. The institution found distinguished headquarters in the *Prinsens Palæ*, a magnificent Rococo-style building erected in the mid-eighteenth century for Frederick V by the king's favorite architect Nicolai Eigtved. The building stands on the other side of the canal from Christiansborg, right in front of the wing that opens onto the Courtyard of the Riding Stables.

This is the country's most important museum and it is divided into several sectors. The *Ethnographic Collection* covers the whole history of Danish civilization from prehistory to our time. It contains authentic artifacts ranging from the first traces left by Man in Danish territories (flints, utensils, etc.) to objects from Viking culture, including the arms, jewels and instru-

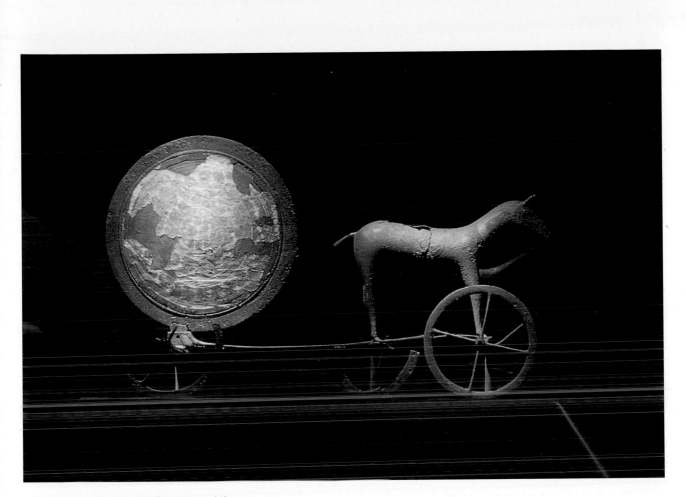

One of the most famous works on view at the Nationalmuseet in the section devoted to the history of Danish civilization. The Sun Chariot, made of gold and bronze, was found in Trundholm and dates back to between 1800 and 1000 BC.

ments (especially the characteristic wind instrument known as the "lur") belonging to the intermediate period. Medieval and Renaissance treasures follow with a rich array of altar pieces and polyptychs, while still other artifacts lead up to the most important expressions of our modern age. The oldest pieces of the *Coin and Medallion Collection* can be traced back to Asia Minor, Greece and Macedonia but there are also examples of coins from all over the world. The *Farming Culture and Civilization Section* mostly studies rural life in Denmark but also in Scandinavia as a whole. The *Greenland Department* displays the costumes, traditions and customs of Eskimo cultures while the *Ethnographic Collections* are devoted to the very different his-

tory and traditions of various geographical areas of the world: from Africa to Indonesia, from India to Amazonia, from Oceania to Japan. The *Egyptian and Classical Antiquities Collection* gathers the innumerable artifacts of great interest that have been uncovered by expeditions of Danish archeologists.

Overall the museum hosts an enormous and inestimable treasure which is arranged not only on the four floors of the original *Prinsens Palæ* but also in another building which, although connecting, has its own separate entrance. The recent renovation of the whole complex has led to a reordering of the collections and the consequent rearrangement of museum displays.

NY CARLSBERG GLYPTOTEK

This is one of the most important ancient art museums in the world but it also boasts the largest collection of French Impressionism outside France. It was founded by two famous Danish art patrons, Carl and Ottilia Jacobsen, who used the considerable profits of the Carlsberg Breweries to fund highly deserving initiatives. In 1888 they donated their private collection to the State which entrusted Jens Vilhelm Dahlerup to design a building where the donation could be displayed to advantage. Located not far from the Tivoli Park, the eclectic and monumental building has a magnificent winter garden protected by a large glass dome. In 1902 the *Ny Carlsberg Foundation* was formed to guarantee adequate financial coverage of the institution even after the death of the husband and wife art patrons. In 1906 Hack Kampmann built the wing for the *ancient art collections*, which are divided into various sections. The *Egyptian section* shows a wide array of objects from small statuary to colossal sculpture groups. The *Middle East, Greek and Roman Art sections* include ancient bronzes and ceramics, Ionic, Doric and Attic sculptures as well as some superb examples of Roman statuary. There is also a great portrait gallery of illustrious figures from Imperial Rome not to mention sections devoted to *Etruscan Art* and *Palmyra*.

However, the **Glyptotek** also boasts priceless collections of *modern art* and, to house these in a

The Ny Carlsberg Glyptotek's large collections of ancient and modern art offer an incomparable range of models that attract students and art lovers from all over the world. Its substantial gallery of masterpieces is displayed in an expert manner.

worthy fashion, a new wing was added to the main building in 1996. The section dedicated to *Impressionism* deserves special note because it amply documents that art movement's entire range of activity with works by Corot, Manet, Géricault, Renoir, Cézanne, Monet, Degas as well as providing an excellent overview of Gauguin's work. Other well-represented artists include Van Gogh, Toulouse-Lautrec, Vuillard and Bonnard while several rooms are devoted to *French sculpture* with works by Rodin, Carpeaux, Maillol, and others. Ample space has been given to paintings and sculptures of the *Danish Art* collection while the section reserved for *European Sculpture* boasts the famous *Three Graces* by Antonio Canova.

The Glyptotek offers a complete panorama ranging from ancient art to the most recent artistic expressions. Below, the famous Mother of the Waters, a work by Danish sculptor Kai Nielsen.

TIVOLI

In the immediate environs of the *Rådhuspladsen*, the beautiful gardens of *H.C. Andersens Boulevard* are a pleasant prelude to the world famous **Tivoli Pleasure Park**. This is a kaleidoscopic mix of amusement park and restaurants, concert halls and stages (such as the one for mimes and the *Chinese Theater*) interspersed with pagodas and brightly-colored fields of flowers. It is all lit up at night by a beautiful myriad of lights and always has a festive and exciting atmosphere. Built in 1843 by Georg Carstensen and later remodeled several times, little remains of the nineteenth-century design although some traces can still be seen in the main entrance and in the small lake which is the last vestige of the ancient bastion's moat. Tivoli also boasts three orchestras — of which one is symphonic — as well as its own guard, in full uniform, made up of boys from 10 to 16 years old. An amazing fireworks display marks the close of almost every full day of fun in the park.

The Arab Palace located in front of the Bubble Fountain.

THE BLACK DIAMOND

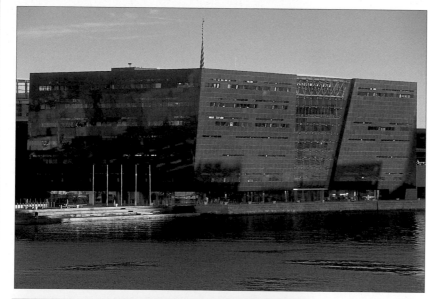

This futuristic building by the architects Schmidt, Hammer, and Lassen, in the shape of an irregular cube with glistening surfaces, is a contemporary-art addition to the port side of the Royal Library. Begun in 1996 and inaugurated on 15 September 1999, the **Black Diamond** has rapidly become one of the liveliest cultural centers in all Copenhagen. Here, besides having access to the incalculable wealth of books and other published matter available in the Library, casual visitors and scholars alike can peruse many different exhibits, attend concerts and meetings, and participate in debates and discussion groups. An association known as the Diamond Club brings together the afficionados of this innovative institution – and a periodical, The Diamond, publishes up-to-date information on all the center's many initiatives.

The contemporary structure of the Black Diamond, a fascinating futuristic addition to the Royal Library.

THE BRIDGE OVER THE ØRESUND

Denmark celebrated the arrival of the Third Millennium with an authentic masterpiece of modern engineering: the futuristic **bridge-tunnel** that spans the wide arm of the Øresund Sea to link Copenhagen and Malmo – Denmark and Sweden. The benefits for the two countries are immediately apparent, but the advantages of the bridge-tunnel in uniting Scandinavia and the rest of the European continent are also considerable.

The new structure, which was officially inaugurated on 1 July 2000, is composed of two sections. The first is a tunnel 3.5 Km in length that dives into the earth at Kastrup, south of the Danish capital, and emerges on an artificial island a little over 4 Km long in the middle of the strait. The second section, an elegant, soaring suspension bridge almost 8 Km long, continues on into Sweden. The whole bridge-tunnel structure is on two levels: a lower level with a double track for trains runs underneath a four-lane highway for vehicle traffic.

The soaring, slender lines of the new bridge that spans the wide arm of the Øresund to link Denmark and Sweden.

THE PLANETARIUM

The brand new **planetarium** could only be named after Denmark's most famous astronomer, Tycho Brahe. It has been built on the shores of the Sankt Jørgens Sø, the westernmost of the city's three artificial lakes. Shows are held here every day, starting at eleven o'clock and continuing hourly. With the aid of film footage and realistic astronomical reconstructions the viewer is projected into the discovery of the universe.

Housed in an unusual and innovative building, the planetarium offers futuristic shows that illustrate the universe around us.

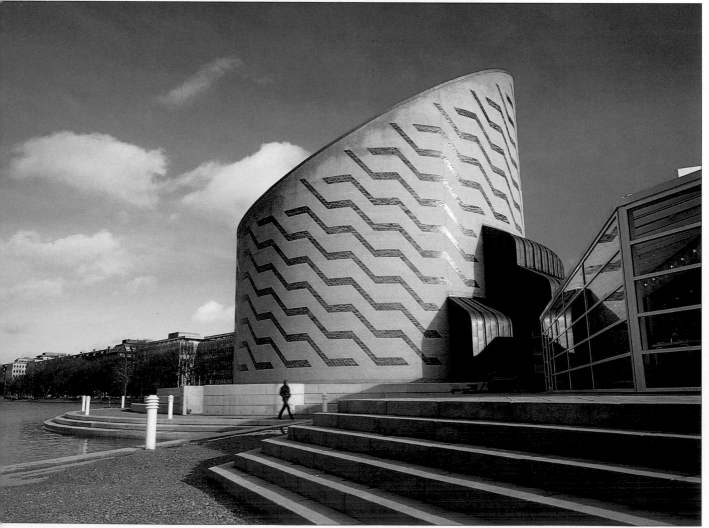

THE 'GREAT LAKES'

To the west of the city center, three contiguous and regularly-shaped artificial bodies of water give the illusion of being a river as they extend over an area of almost three kilometers. Dug to ensure a drinking water reserve for the city and to ward off attack on the west side, **Sortedamns Sø**, **Peblinge Sø** and **Sankt Jørgens Sø** today offer walkers an inviting shoreline where they can observe seabirds building their nests. Not far from here rises the modern architecture of the **Parken Stadium**, the great venue for soccer matches.

The green area around the lakes, with the nearby stadium (top) and the famous Søpavillon (right).

The elegant and stately Rosenborg Slot, with its fine gateway for the Guard Corps. A monument in the royal garden commemorates Huns Christian Andersen.

ROSENBORG

Although the **Rosenborg Slot**'s moat and drawbridge could lead one to suppose that it was a stalwart fortification, Christian IV had it built between 1606 and 1633 as a pleasure pavilion in the middle of the magnificent **Kongens Have** garden. The oldest in the city, the garden was designed in 1606 for the same king and today is a beautiful and popular public park. As for the original building, it was much smaller than it is today. It has grown over time with the addition of other rooms and of towers, among which the octagonal one that — curiously enough — contains the stairway. However the castle was only really used as a royal residence during its first hundred years then it gradually became a lavish storage space for precious treasures belonging to the Crown. In this way the _Rosenborg Slot_ became the museum it is today. Its innumerable apartments contain rich reconstructions of different period rooms as they would have been furnished under various kings, not to mention wonderful collections of jewels, ceramics and glassware.

Although it has been enlarged several times, the Rosenborg Slot has preserved its balanced and uniform appearance which is characterized by a number of towers, including the octagonal one that encloses the stairs. At the center of this page, the great Gallery where three silver lions by F. Küblich stand guard over the two golden royal thrones.

THE CROWN JEWELS

Among Rosenborg's many treasures, the most precious are undoubtedly the **Crown Jewels**. Displayed in a special room, these include the two royal crowns (one used in the period of absolute monarchy and the other for the constitutional monarchy) as well as an array of splendid and priceless works in gold, pearls and precious stones.

46

Views of the magnificent Botanical Garden's thriving flora as well as the elegant tower of the Palmhuset, the greenhouse for tropical plants.
Lower right, the monument to Tycho Brahe, the famous Danish astronomer, stands in front of the old Astronomical Observatory of Copenhagen.

THE BOTANICAL GARDEN

On the site where in ancient times city fortifications had been erected, a vast **Botanical Garden** (*Botanisk Have*) was built, between 1871 and 1874, over an area of almost ten hectares. The garden continues to collect plants and flowers of many different, and sometimes rare, species. Special attention is given, obviously, to Danish flora but there are also more unusual specimens, from Greenland and from the Fær Øer archipelago. Rising above the statues and fountains that adorn the whole complex, the *Palmhuset*, a grandiose greenhouse built in 1874, was designed to shelter tropical plants that otherwise couldn't survive in Copenhagen's climate. Nearby there are other buildings devoted to research and study including an *astronomical observatory* and the Geological Museum, *Geologisk Museum*, which houses an interesting collection of meteorites.

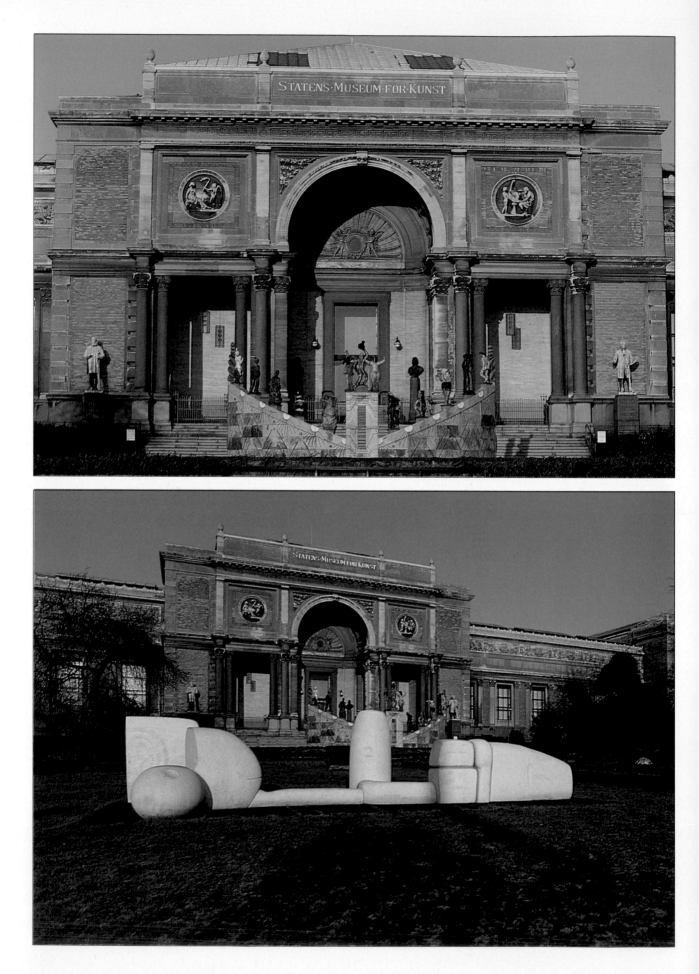

STATENS MUSEUM FOR KUNST

I n 1896 Jens Vilhelm Dahlerup erected an original and eclectic-style building that would house the royal painting collections which had been deprived of an exhibition space in the great Christiansborg fire of 1884. Today Dahlerup's building, extended and renovated several times during the twentieth century to increase its capacity and functionality, hosts the works of the **Statens Museum for Kunst**. Originating from that first core of royal collections, today the works are so numerous — indeed, with its over ten thousand pieces, it is the richest collection in all of Scandinavia — that they cannot all be exhibited in the building's more than one hundred rooms. Thus every year Danish, Scandinavian, Dutch, Flemish and Italian art from the 1600s to today is shown on a rotating basis, including works by some of the great masters from Dürer to Rembrandt, from Picasso to Matisse, from Tintoretto to Titian, from Munch to Rubens.

A wonderful eclectic façade is a prelude to the Statens Museum for Kunst's extremely elegant yet functional interior arrangement that is well suited to organizing important shows of Danish, Scandinavian and European art.

AMALIENBORG

Queen Margaret and her family normally reside at the elegant and monumental **Amalienborg** complex. After the blaze that devastated Christiansborg, these four symmetrical buildings (made up of a central core and two side wings, arranged around an eight-sided square) were made into a single royal residence in 1794, during the reign of Christian VII. However they had all been built previously, between 1750 and 1768 in a typical Rococo style, by one architect, Nicolai Eigtved, who had been commissioned by four different aristocratic families whose names are still used to distinguish the buildings: the *Brockdorff Palœ*, *Levetzau Palœ* (the Queen Mother's residence), *Moltke Palœ* (used for ceremonies and official receptions) and the *Schack-Løvenskjold Palœ* (the Queen's home and when she is in residence the royal banner flies from this building's flagpole). The last two palaces are joined by a passage fronted by a *Neoclassical colonnade* (*Kolonnaden*), an eighteenth-century work by Caspar Frederik Harsdorff. This leads onto the south side of the square where the *equestrian statue of Frederick V* stands, a work by Jacques François Joseph Saly (1754-1771). The interiors of the four buildings making up the Amalienborg complex are remarkable for the elegance and refinement of

Beautiful views of the four sister buildings at Amalienborg, the royal residence located near the port and separated from it by the luxurious Amaliehaven gardens. The equestrian monument of Frederick V dominates the center of the vast octagonal-shaped square.

Some views of the sober but very refined rooms of the Amalienborg royal palace, the official residence of the Queen and her family. Priceless examples of the famous Danish Royal Porcelain are displayed here.

their furnishings. The *Levetzau Palæ* in particular houses an interesting exhibition: *De Danske Kongers Kronologiske Samling* is entirely devoted to both the day-to-day life and the official engagements of the members of the Danish royal family in the nineteenth and twentieth centuries. Here in display cases one can admire jewels, silver, porcelain as well as costumes and dress, small curiosities that allow us to enter — on tiptoe — into the more private, though royal, affairs of a ruling dynasty.

THE CHANGING OF THE GUARD

Every day at noon a characteristic event brings curious passers-by and tourists to the eight-sided square at Amalienborg. This is where the spectacular **Vagtparade** takes place, the ceremony of the changing of the guard. When the Queen is in residence the change is solemnly marked by music from a military band. From the *Rosenborg Have* barracks, near the castle of the same name, the soldiers of the Royal Guard (*Den Kongelige Livgarde*) march here in their unmistakable uniforms and helmets and proceed with the customary maneuvers which last a good half hour and are thoroughly enjoyed by spectators of all ages.

The soldiers of the Royal Guards in their characteristic uniforms and helmets are the ones to watch at the Changing of the Guard ceremony that takes place in the square of Amalienborg.

AMALIEHAVEN

The splendid garden of **Amaliehaven** extends east of Amalienborg in the direction of the port. Designed by the Belgian architect Delonge, it was donated to the city of Copenhagen in 1983 by the A.P. Møller Foundation that had undertaken the restoration of the old port district. In the middle of the garden a circular *fountain* is located on an axis with the statue in the Amalienborg square. Watching over the fountain are four original, vertical *sculptures* which, together with the interesting *fountains* at the north and south ends of the park, are works by Arnaldo Pomodoro.

FREDERIKS KIRKEN

Located west of Amalienborg and better known as the "Marble Church" (*Marmorkirken*), the **Frederiks Kirken** with its imposing dome was designed by Nicolai Eigtved for Frederick V who was engaged in the grandiose project of rebuilding and renovating "his" city. Building began in 1749 but was only completed in 1894 thanks to the concrete interest taken by the art patron C.F. Tietgen and the work of the architect Ferdinand Mehldal. Construction had been interrupted for over a century due to the lack of funds, and this had led to the almost total ruin of the parts that had already been built. Carried out in white Norwegian marble, the church has a round plan and is noteworthy for its monumental *colonnade* and for the gates surrounding the building, adorned with *statues* of some of the most important members of the Danish Church. Other *statues* of biblical figures are seen along the balustrade of the copper-roofed *dome* which soars almost fifty meters and is clearly inspired by Roman models. Inside, the dome is decorated with *frescoes* of enormous figures of the *Apostles* painted by Christen Nielsen Overgård and Henrik Olrik.

Left, sculptures and original fountains created by Arnaldo Pomodoro for the garden of Amaliehaven. Right, a majestic dome tops the Frederiks Kirken.

Copenhagen's large mercantile port has recently opened to cruise ships as well. Over the last twenty years, a whole series of new buildings, of impressive architectural stature, have been constructed in the port district.

THE PORT

The fortunes of the city of Copenhagen have always been tied to the presence of a very active **port**. Today, after going through a period of decline in maritime traffic and a consequently strong depression, this imposing port has been thoroughly revitalized, not only from a strictly commercial point of view (to the north the *free port zone* is still active) but also as a landing for ferries and cruise liners (about two hundred tour ships pass through here every year). Even the old piers and warehouses that had literally been abandoned for many years have recently been renovated and made into offices as part of a general rehabilitation project for the whole port area. New buildings have been erected as well: some of these are residential (providing the extraordinary opportunity of living on the sea while in the middle of a port!) while others serve as headquarters for different maritime companies. Thus the whole area has taken on new life; it has regained an important place within the city plan as well as an architectural dignity that had been lost for many years.

Views of the royal fleet and landing dock: above, the luxurious "Dannebrog" that the Queen uses for her trips by sea.

THE ROYAL FLEET

In a country that has always lived in close contact with the sea, the royal family has to have a suitable fleet. It is headed up by what could be called another official residence: the magnificent ship "Dannebrog" used by the Queen and her family to set out by sea to visit not only various Danish cities but even remote destinations as far away as Greenland.

LANGELINIE

The great project to restore the vast port area began in the early 1980s and brought about some interesting results. One of these was the addition to the *Havnepromenade* ("the port walkway" which had already been developed in the 1970s) of the **Langelinie**, the beautiful pathway along the shore that leads to the tourist wharfs and the free port. Walking along it one encounters famous monuments like the *Little Mermaid* and the *statue dedicated to Mamma Bear*, as well as impressive, historic buildings like the old fortified bastion known as the Kastellet. This citadel, built in 1640 for Christian IV, was meant to be the eastern-most bulwark of the fortified walls that the king wanted to erect around the city. With reconstruction under Frederick III in the second half of the seventeenth century, the **Kastellet** took on the pentagonal form that still distinguishes it today, extending over an area of twenty hectares. Although most of the fortifications were torn down during the nineteenth century, the citadel which has been converted into a park, still preserves the large courtyard and barracks used by the garrison guard and its officers. Instead, Christian IV offered the characteristic area of **Nyboder** to the Navy's use and one can still see there the low buildings in perfect rows as well as the more cheerful gardens. It is interesting to note that today the houses are two storeys high because they were raised during the eighteenth century.

THE GEFION FOUNTAIN

Not far from *Nyboder* is the **Gefion Springvandet**, a monumental fountain created in 1908 by Anders Bundgård and inspired by Norse mythology. In fact the majestic group of bronze figures features the goddess Gefion who, according to legend, was born in Norway. This divinity was sent to earth by Odin where, through her persuasive ways, she was able to secure from the Swedish king Gylfe the gift of all the earth she could plough in one day. The goddess transformed her four sons into oxen and succeeded in ploughing the better part of the country. This story explains the origin of the great Swedish lake of *Vanern* while the vast piece of earth that had been dug out was said to have landed in the Baltic Sea where it formed the island of *Sjælland*.

Upper left, the characteristic Nyboder quarter that Christian IV (portrayed in the statue seen in the photo) built for members of the Navy; (center) the large military quarters still seen inside the Kastellet; (right) the Gefion Fountain in all its stately beauty is located near Skt. Alban Kirke, the only Anglican Church in Copenhagen.

THE LITTLE MERMAID

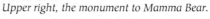

Atrue symbol of Copenhagen and of Denmark as a whole, the world famous **Little Mermaid** (*Lille Havfrue*) watches the sea from a rock at the entrance to the port. The statue was made in 1913 by Edvard Eriksen who was inspired by one of the most melancholic but best-loved characters from Hans Christian Andersen's fairy tales: the young mermaid who chooses to die for love of a handsome prince.

Walking along the Langelinie, one comes across the Little Mermaid, resting on her rock. With a melancholy countenance, she gazes out to sea and to the horizon.
Upper right, the monument to Mamma Bear.

THE BEACHES

The climate in Denmark is cold in the winter and extremely rainy in the summer. So it is hardly surprising that the residents of Copenhagen all share a great wish for sun and on fine summer days the **beaches of Charlottenlund** are always crowded. Located just north of the city center and not far from the large aquarium, this strip of sand along the Øresund is a public beach where the Danes' desire for direct contact with nature means that the number of facilities available, including changing rooms and umbrellas, has been reduced to a minimum.

An incredible number of people flock to beaches around Copenhagen in the summertime. Changing rooms and umbrellas are hardly ever used because they get in the way of a freer and more direct contact with the natural environment.

DINING IN COPENHAGEN

Although characterized by simple dishes derived from the country's farming and fishing traditions, Danish cuisine is extremely varied. Fish, either steamed or baked, abound on Copenhagen's tables, while smoked herrings are considered a specialty. More finicky diners can try the eels or shrimps fished in Danish seas and sometimes prepared with eggs and vegetables. However, other foods are equally popular, from cheeses (the local varieties are excellent whether they are fresh or aged) to potatoes, from beef to pork (either roasted or smoked), to typical cold dishes like the *smørrebrød* – the very popular and highly garnished sandwiches arranged on generously-buttered black bread. Among the incomparable sweets, Danish apple fritters are world famous. All is washed down by the ubiquitous drink of choice: beer. Among the most important traditional specialties, the classic pea soup is highly seasoned. Pork, too, is the basis for a wide range of common dishes, usually accompanied by potatoes or cabbage prepared in a variety of ways. To end on a high note, there is nothing better than an aquavitae or a drop of the classic currant liqueur.

Frederiksberg Slot is situated at the center of a vast park; here, among canals, lakes and delightful pavilions (left, the Chinese Pavilion) people enjoy relaxing and sometimes even sunbathing.

FREDERIKSBERG

To the west of Copenhagen's historic center lies the large park of **Frederiksberg Have**, laid out in the 1700s by Johan Cornelius Krieger and adorned with statues and *pavilions*, among which the most famous is the *Chinese Pavilion*. Residents of Copenhagen delight in its lake and system of canals and enjoy relaxing in this oasis of greenery. Situated at the center of the park, the **Frederiksberg Slot** is an austere building that was erected by King Frederick IV who, during a trip to Italy, had been deeply struck by the architecture of villas, especially the ones in Frascati. The architect was Ernst Brandenburger who, between 1699 and 1703, carried out his design which foresaw only the central body of the building. The two side wings were added between 1733 and 1738 by Laurids de Thurah.

THE ZOO

Among the oldest zoological gardens in the world, Copenhagen's **Zoologisk Have** at the gates of the Frederiksberg castle hosts over two thousand animals. It has recently been renovated to improve its facilities and to diversify their functions, as well as to create a *learning zoo* for children. From the top of the high *tower* (built in 1905 and more then 40 meters high) overlooking the zoo entrance, the magnificent panorama embraces even the coast of Sweden.

The top of the high tower rising above the Zoo entrance as well as photographs of some of the delightful animals that can be seen there.

THE ENVIRONS

DRAGØR

The picturesque fishing town of **Dragør** lies just south of Copenhagen and *Amager Island*. It is particularly delightful and welcoming with its distinctive small yellow and white houses covered with tiled roofs, laid out in perfect rows along carefully cobblestoned streets. Already during the Middle Ages, a rather important port for herring fishery existed in this area but the town's good fortune really began in the 1500s when Christian II donated vast territories of *Amager Island* to a colony of Dutch farmers. In return they farmed the area and provided the king's court with fresh

vegetables and flowers. From that time for the next three hundred years, *Dragør* underwent continual development, acquiring the characteristic town plan that still distinguishes it today.

One of the oldest buildings in the town now houses the *Dragør Museum*; interesting collections of clothing, furniture and drawings as well as models of boats and their equipment aim to offer a wide-ranging yet detailed look at the history, economic resources and traditions of this small city. Nearby another *museum* has been devoted to the painter Christian Mølsted, a famous local artist.

The typical architecture of Dragør: white and yellow houses and perfectly cobbled streets.

NORTH-WEST OF COPENHAGEN

The *Bispebjerg* district north-west of Copenhagen is famous above all for the **Grundtvigs Kirke**, a church that is unmistakable for its peculiar architecture. It was conceived as a monument to the memory of Nicolai Grundtvig, a key member of the Danish Protestant Church who died 1872. He was particularly beloved for his dedication to the cause of widespread schooling, even among the poorer social classes. Construction of the new church designed by Jensen Klint was begun in 1921 on an area donated by the city of Copenhagen and with state funding as well as with contributions raised during a special campaign. Its execution was entrusted to six of the most expert masons in all Denmark who used over six million yellow bricks and took almost twenty years to complete the building. The result is clearly inspired by the rural churches and their characteristic Romanesque-Gothic style found throughout Denmark. Its extremely original form — with the impressive façade tower and enormous triangular porch over the entrance — recalls an enormous pipe organ. Indeed, the church's interior, which also shows marked Gothic elongation, hosts one of the largest organs in all Scandinavia, built in 1965, with over four thousand pipes.

The Grundtvigs Kirke's distinctive tower.

THE KAREN BLIXEN MUSEUM

I n *Rungsted*, north of Copenhagen and not far from *Helsingør*, lies the great **estate** of *Rungstedlund Fuglereservat* where Karen Blixen retired to spend the last years of her life. Apart from being a great Danish writer, she was a courageous and strong-willed woman who had a deep love for Africa where she lived for many years and her story has been brought to world attention by a recent hit film. She wrote in her will that, upon her death, the vast Rungstedlund property should be made into a *wildlife reserve*, and it was in the heart of this reserve that she chose to be

The splendid Rungsted estate, today converted into a wildlife reserve, includes the house where Karen Blixen spent the last years of her life and the park where she chose to be buried.

buried. As for the large house, in the 1980s it was converted into a *museum*. Here, together with the elegant and tastefully furnished rooms that are perfectly preserved, many objects that the writer brought back from Africa are carefully displayed: further evidence of her deep and nostalgic bond to that land, a bond which, even over a great distance, after her return to Denmark, could never be severed.

The rooms inside the large house, today a museum, contain many objects and souvenirs brought directly from Africa.

KRONBORG SLOT

The famous castle of Elsinore, the setting for Shakespeare's Hamlet, is better known in Denmark as the **Kronborg Slot**. It overlooks the port of Helsingør on the Øresund, not far from the shores of Sweden to which it is connected by a frequent ferry service. The city was already fortified in the 1200s but in the next century it was conquered by the armies of the Hanseatic League. The castle, rising above the point that closes the eastern tip of the port, was rebuilt and refurbished in 1420 by order of Henry VII of Pomerania. From here the ruler could levy duties on all the ships sailing through the strait and this taxation would continue down to 1857. Later the impressive building was renovated under Frederick II who entrusted the work

(1574-1577) to the Dutch architect Jan van Pæschen. However, construction would only be completed in 1585 under the supervision of Anthonis van Opbergen. Seriously damaged by a 1629 fire, the castle was definitively rebuilt in the following decades. In the 1600s incursions by Swedish troops deprived the castle of its valuable art collections. All the same Kronborg Slot is still one of the most magnificent Danish homes, protected as it is by a double ring of walls and moats and topped by the elegant profiles of corner towers as well as the more central and highest *Tower of the Trumpeters*. It is well worth a visit to the beautiful *chapel* with its three naves where, among Renaissance furnishings, one can admire the *royal gallery* in sculpted wood and the

Kronborg Slot, the heavily fortified castle surrounded by bastions, has some unique architectural elements like its severe façades, impressive corner towers, and the elegant Tower of the Trumpeters that soars above the rest. Three orders of windows as well as characteristic dormers face onto the rectangular courtyard.

Some light-filled rooms of the royal apartments, furnished in a sober, elegant style. (On the previous page, above, the room known as the Great Hall.)
This page, above, the chapel with the prominent royal gallery in carved wood.
Below, Holger Danske, the sleeping Viking of mythology

sixteenth-century altar in marble and alabaster. The elegant *royal apartments*, ceremonial halls, rooms reserved for important guests, as well as the king's wing and the queen's apartments are all decorated with ancient fireplaces, tapestries, antique furniture and a fascinating picture gallery. In the keeps stands a statue of *Holger Danske*, the mythological Viking chief who, as legend tells, has been sleeping for centuries but, in times of danger, is ready to wake up to defend Denmark. So it was not by chance that Holger's name was used as a password by the Danish Resistance during the Second World War.

LOUISIANA

Of all of Denmark's modern art museums, *Louisiana* located just outside *Helsingør* (in the coastal suburb of *Humlebæk*, to be precise) enjoys a well-deserved international reputation. Housed in a building with many rooms joined by a series of corridors, the museum hosts many temporary exhibitions every year. It has a remarkable permanent collection that includes all different kinds of artistic expressions from painting to sculpture, from prints to photography. Among the almost five hundred works on view, there are many important pieces of Danish art by artists like Karl Isakson, Erik Hoppe and Asger Jorn as well as a permanent exhibition of work by the CoBrA group. But European art is also brilliantly represented with pieces by Picasso, Dubuffet and Kandinsky to name just a few; there are twelve bronze statues by Alberto Giacometti and three large sculptures by Henry Moore. Even the large park surrounding the museum and running down to the sea has been transformed into a wonderful exhibition space. Near the seashore a café-restaurant has been set up and the large *Character*, a bronze by Joan Miró, sits on the lawn in front of it, just one example of the intelligent use of display spaces that is really one of the hallmarks of this museum.

In displaying its masterpieces, Louisiana, one of the greatest Danish museums of modern art, has used even outdoor spaces to great effect.

Views of the stupendous Jægersborg Dyrehave park where deer roam free in the shade of stately, centuries-old trees.

JÆGERSBORG DYREHAVE

On the shore of the Øresund, in an area full of especially fine residential developments, the vast park of **Jægersborg Dyrehave** is famous for the many deer that graze here under the shade of centuries-old trees. Indeed even the park's origins date back to rather ancient times, to its creation in the thirteenth century by King Valdemar II. Every year,

The Eremitageslot, the great hunting lodge built by Christian VI right in the middle of the park.

EREMITAGESLOT

just before winter, *Jægersborg Dyrehave* hosts a rather curious hunt where the prey is actually a rider who is chased by hunters on horseback through a specially-designed obstacle course.

To the south of *Jægersborg Dyrehave*, **Dyrehavs-bakken** is one of the country's oldest amusement parks, boasting many very popular attractions.

Another king, Christian VI, who wanted to enjoy the marvels of *Jægersborg* more fully, commissioned the elegant hunting lodge known as **Eremitage-slot**, built in the center of the park in 1736 by Laurids de Thurah. An example of Late Baroque architecture, it still stands, in its austere but elegant form, surrounded by the intense green of the splendid estate.

FREDENSBORG

Less than fifty kilometers from Copenhagen, the small city of Fredensborg owes its fame to its majestic **Royal Palace**. Frederick IV had it built in 1740 to mark the peace agreement with Sweden, Denmark's historic enemy, so it is not a coincidence that *Fredensborg Slot* is also known as the Castle of Peace. It was designed by Johan Cornelius Krieger who strictly adhered to the canons of Italian architecture. Later the whole building underwent various renovations which did not, however, substantially modify its appearance. This was Frederick V's favorite castle where, in the large gardens, he arranged sculptures of common people, mostly farmers and fishermen, portrayed in the typical costumes of the area. *Fredensborg Slot* soon replaced the nearby castle of Frederiksborg, both in its function and importance. Even today the queen's family comes here to stay, usually in the summertime, so the building is open to the visiting public only in certain periods of the year.

A wide octagonal courtyard flanked by service buildings leads to the royal palace itself which is topped by a tall domed structure that covers a wide ceremonial hall. To the right of the main body of the building, we find some elegant appendices in the magnificent *Royal Chapel*, the *stables*, and a building which, although historically used to house officers of the Guard, has recently been renovated and con-

A wide tree-lined avenue leads to the large octagonal courtyard in front of the magnificent royal home at Fredensborg. The rectangular main building is seen here with the unique domed construction that rises above it.

verted into a residence for the Queen Mother. The eighteenth-century interiors, still elegantly furnished, are particularly beautiful, sometimes tending towards Neoclassicism, at others towards Rococo. A magnificent *park*, laid out under the supervision of Johan Cornelius Krieger himself, extends all around the great complex, reaching even as far as Lake Esrum.

Fredensborg is famous for its rich Neoclassical and Rococo interiors, where paintings and tapestries form the backdrop to exceptional eighteenth-century furnishings. On the following page, the photo in the upper left gives an idea of the huge dimensions of the superb ceremonial hall located under Fredensborg's dome.

FRILANDSMUSEET

The result of a careful restoration, **Frilandsmuseet** north of *Lyngby* is one of the largest outdoor museums in Northern Europe, extending over almost forty hectares. It brings together a number of typical buildings from Germany and Sweden as well as from Denmark, all dating from the seventeenth to the nineteenth century. The constructions have been dismantled and transferred from their original location to this park where they have been put back together. Afterwards, they are furnished with pieces that strictly respect the periods and the geographical area of each building. Mills and farms, factories and humble lodgings have the chance to stand out in this environment which has been so carefully preserved and protected.

A stupendous natural setting, among mills and farms, is undoubtedly one of the attractions of the Frilandsmuseet.

FREDERIKSBORG

The stately complex of the *Frederiksborg Castle* is one of the most beautiful royal homes of Denmark, with its flowering of towers, timpani and spires. It was erected on a very unusual site: on three small islands in the middle of a large channel, in the city of *Hillerød*, about forty kilometers northwest of Copenhagen. The original body of the castle was acquired in 1560 by Frederick II who immediately began to enlarge it by erecting two twin circular towers. But the building in its present form owes more to Christian IV, the Architect King, who was born here and who, between 1605 and 1621, did everything in his power to enlarge, embellish, modify and renovate the structure following the dictates of the Renaissance style. It underwent modernization between 1736 and 1740, especially in the living quarters, only to be almost completely destroyed again in an 1859 fire that left only the chapel unscathed. The castle was rebuilt in just six years, following the original design and with funds obtained through a national campaign. Today the castle is the distinguished headquarters of the **Museum of Danish National History** which was created in 1878 with the patronage of the Carlsberg Foundation, founded by the beer manufacturer Carl Jacobsen. The many priceless works of art preserved here make a visit well worthwhile.

The center of the castle is reached by traversing two islands, passing through two fortified gates and a quadrangular keep and crossing a wide courtyard where the hexagonal *Fountain of Neptune* (*Neptunspringevandet*) is situated. The bronze figures adorning it are nineteenth-century copies since the originals

The majestic castle of Frederiksborg, erected on three small islands, is characterized by its many towers (the highest of which is the bell tower), pinnacles, spires and dormers.

Views showing the complex structure of the castle which was erected inside a moat. Behind the Neptune Fountain, the façades of two side wings are connected by a blind colonnade with niches containing statues.

Even Frederiksborg's interior spaces are remarkable for their splendor. Of particular interest is the immense Hall of the Knights (above), used for dancing and site of the Trumpeters' Gallery, not to mention the superb chapel (right) which for centuries hosted the coronation ceremony of Danish kings and which was the only part of the castle to survive the 1859 fire.

were carried off by Swedish troops in 1659 and can still be seen in Drottingsholm, not far from Stockholm. As for the castle interior, there are two beautiful *wings* reserved respectively for the sovereign and her children. Particularly noteworthy are the *Council Hall*, the *Hall of the Knights* and the chapel known as *Slotskirke* where, for two hundred years, the coronation ceremony of Danish kings was held. Here one can admire the great seventeenth-century *organ*, a masterpiece by Esajas Compenius of Braunschweig as well as the stucco ornaments of the vault and the coat-of-arms of Christian IV and his consort Anna Caterina which still rise above the three sunlit Renaissance naves.

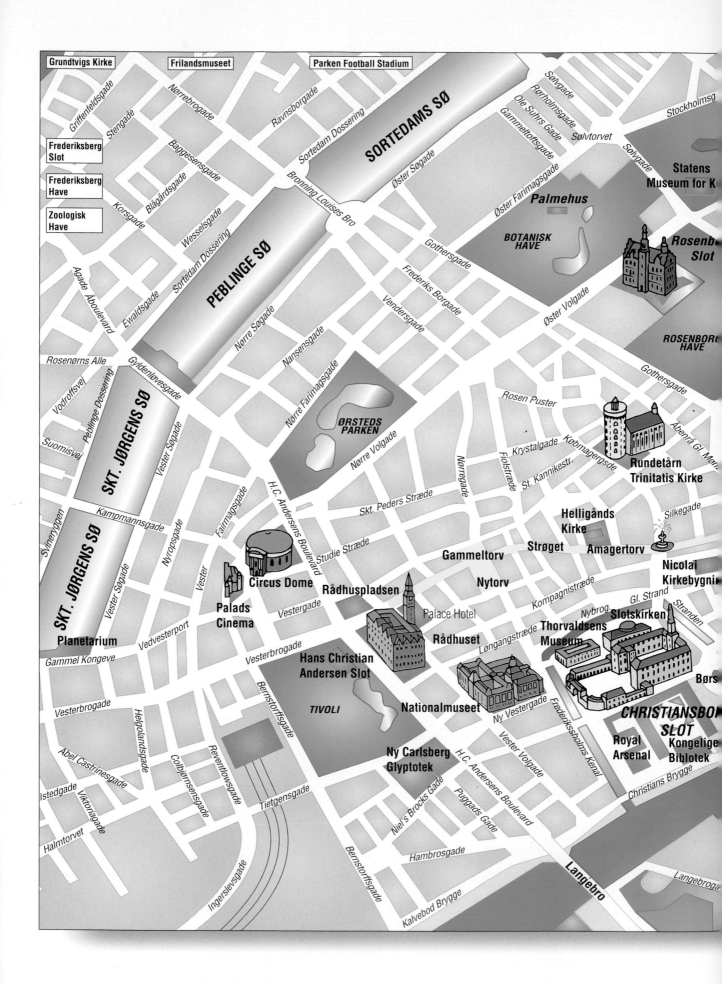

Grundtvigs Kirke

Frilandsmuseet

Parken Football Stadium

Frederiksberg Slot

Frederiksberg Have

Zoologisk Have

Griffenfeldsgade

Stengade

Nørrebrogade

Ravnsborgade

SORTEDAMS SØ

Sølvgade

Rørholmsgade

Ole Suhrs Gade

Gammeltoftsgade

Stockholmsg.

Sølvtorvet

Sølvgade

Statens Museum for K

Baggesensgade

Sortedam Dossering

Øster Søgade

Øster Farimagsgade

Palmehus

Rosenb Slot

Frederiksberg Slot

Blågårdsgade

Wesselsgade

Bronning Louises Bro

Gothersgade

BOTANISK HAVE

Korsgade

PEBLINGE SØ

Frederiks Borgade

ROSENBOR HAVE

Agade Åboulevard

Sortedam Dossering

Ewaldsgade

Nørre Søgade

Nansensgade

Vendersgade

Øster Volgade

Gothersgade

Rosenørns Alle

Gyldenløvesgade

Nørre Farimagsgade

Rosen Puster

Rundetårn

Trinitatis Kirke

Åbenrå Gl. Mon.

Vodroffsvej

Peblinge Dossering

SKT. JØRGENS SØ

Vester Søgade

ØRSTEDS PARKEN

Krystalgade

Købmagergade

Suomisvej

Nørre Volgade

Fiolstræde

St. Kannikestr.

Helligånds Kirke

Silkegade

Kampmannsgade

Nyropsgade

Skt. Peders Stræde

Nørregade

Strøget

Amagertorv

SKT. JØRGENS SØ

Svineryggen

H.C. Andersens Boulevard

Studie Stræde

Gammeltorv

Nicolai Kirkebygni

Vester Søgade

Fairmagsgade

Circus Dome

Nytorv

Kompagnistræde

Gl. Strand

Palads Cinema

Vester

Rådhuspladsen

Palace Hotel

Nybrog.

Slotskirken

Planetarium

Vedvesterport

Vestergade

Rådhuset

Thorvaldsens Museum

Stranden

Gammel Kongeve

Vesterbrogade

Hans Christian Andersen Slot

Løngangstræde

Børs

Vesterbrogade

Bernstorffsgade

TIVOLI

Nationalmuseet

Ny Vestergade

CHRISTIANSBO SLOT

Helgolandsgade

Ny Carlsberg Glyptotek

Vester Volgade

Frederiksholms Kenal

Royal Arsenal

Kongelige Biblotek

Abel Castrinesgade

Colbjørnsensgade

Reventlowsgade

H.C. Andersens Boulevard

Christians Brygge

Istedgade

Viktoriagade

Niel's Brocks Gade

Pluggads Gade

Halmtorvet

Tietgensgade

Hambrosgade

Langebro

Langebroga

Ingerslevsgade

Bernstorffsgade

Kalvebod Brygge

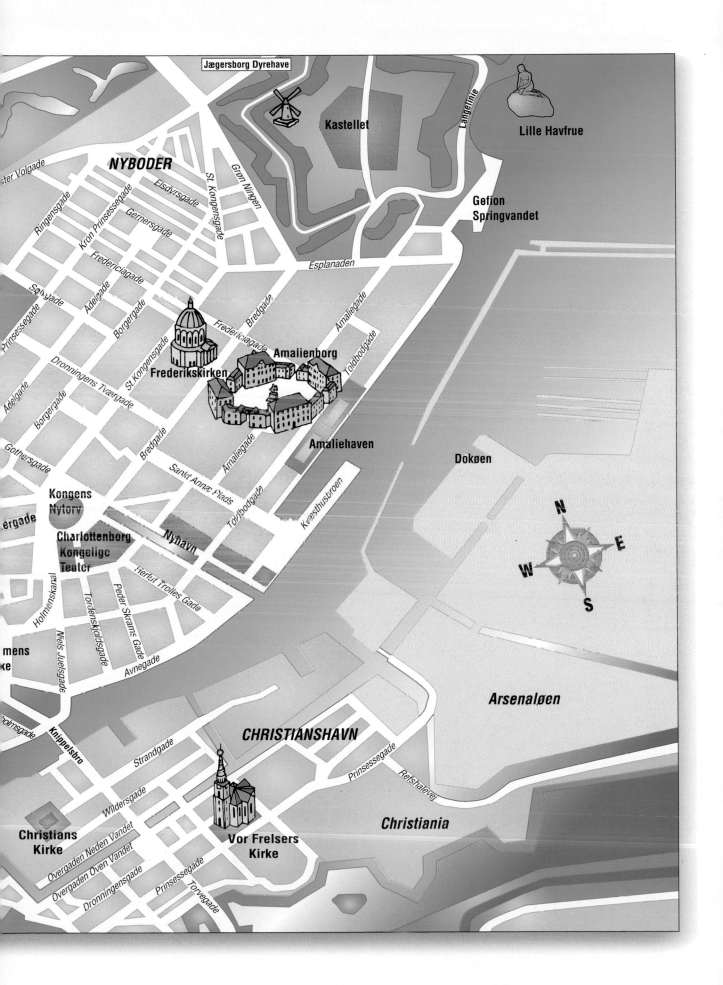

Jægersborg Dyrehave

Kastellet

Langelinie

Lille Havfrue

NYBODER

Øster Volgade

Ringensgade

Krøn Prinsessegade

Elsdvrsgade

Gernersgade

St. Kongensgade

Grøn Ningen

Fredericiagade

Sølvgade

Adelgade

Borgergade

Prinsessegade

St. Kongensgade

Dronningens Tværgade

Gefion
Springvandet

Esplanaden

Bredgade

Fredericiagade

Amaliegade

Amalienborg

Toldbodgade

Frederikskirken

Adelgade

Borgergade

Bredgade

Amaliegade

Amaliehaven

Dokøen

Gothersgade

Sankt Anne Plads

Toldbodgade

Kvæsthusbroen

Kongens
Nytorv

ergade

Charlottenborg
Kongelige
Teater

Nyhavn

Herlut Trolles Gade

Holmenskanal

Peder Skrams Gade

Niels Juelsgade

Tordenskjoldsgade

Avnegade

mens
ke

N

W   E

S

Arsenaløen

holmsgade

Knippelsbro

CHRISTIANSHAVN

Strandgade

Prinsessegade

Refshalevej

Wildersgade

Christians
Kirke

Overgaden Neden Vandet

Vor Frelsers
Kirke

Christiania

Overgaden Oven Vandet

Dronningensgade

Prinsessegade

Torvegade

INDEX